Too much talk
and other stories

The lion and the hare page 2

The wolf and the seven little kids page 9

Too much talk page 17

HELEN MARRON
BOOKMARK
☏ 01213130256

Nelson

The lion and the hare

One day a lion found a little hare.
"I am hungry. You will make
a good dinner," said the lion.
He picked up the hare and
began to carry her to his den.

Just then he saw a big stag run by.
"That stag will make a better dinner
than a little hare," said the lion.
So he dropped the little hare and
ran after the stag.

The stag ran very fast.
He knew that the lion
was just behind him.
He knew the lion wanted to eat him.

The lion could not run
as fast as the stag.
Soon the stag was so far away that
the lion couldn't see him.
"I shall go back and eat the hare,"
said the lion.

The lion had run a long way.
Now he was tired.
He walked slowly back
to the place where
he had dropped the hare.

When he got there, the hare had gone.
The lion was very, very hungry now.
"If I had not been greedy and
run after that stag, I would not be
so hungry now," he said.

"I was silly to run after the big stag when I could have had the little hare for my dinner.
I wanted too much and now
I have nothing."

Be content with what you have.

The wolf and the seven little kids

Mother Goat said one day, "I must go out. Don't let anyone into the house."
"No, we won't," said the seven little kids and they shut the door tight.
The big bad wolf saw Mother Goat leave the house.
"Now is my chance," he said.
"I will eat up the seven little kids."

He tapped on the door. Tap. Tap. Tap.
"Who is that?" said the little kids.
"This is your mother,"
said the big bad wolf.
"Open the door and let me in."
"You are not our mother,"
said the little kids.
"Your voice is too gruff.
Our mother's voice is
soft and sweet.
You are the big bad wolf.
We won't let you in."

So the big bad wolf went away.
He went to his house and
ate a pot of honey.
Then he went back to
Mother Goat's house.
He tapped on the door. Tap. Tap. Tap.
"Who is that?" said the little kids.
"This is your mother,"
said the big bad wolf in a sweet voice.
"Open the door and let me in."

The smallest kid opened the door
a tiny crack.
He saw a big brown foot and
he slammed the door shut.
"You are not our mother,"
said the little kids.
"Your foot is brown.
Our mother's foot is white.
You are the big bad wolf.
We won't let you in."

So the wolf went back to
his house and he dipped
his foot in a bag of white flour.
Then he hopped back to
Mother Goat's house.
He tapped on the door. Tap. Tap. Tap.
"Who is that?" said the little kids.
"This is your mother,"
said the big bad wolf in a sweet voice.
"Open the door and let me in."
"Show us your foot," said the little kids.

So the wolf stuck his white foot round the door and the little kids opened the door wide.
The wolf jumped into the house and ate up all but one of the little kids.
The smallest kid had climbed into the water tub and the wolf did not see him.

Soon Mother Goat came home.
The door was wide open and
there were no little kids.
"Where are my kids?" she cried.
"The big bad wolf must have eaten them all."
Just then the smallest kid
jumped out of the water tub.
He told Mother Goat all about
the big bad wolf.
"I will teach that wolf a lesson," she said.

She went into the forest and
found the wolf fast asleep under a tree.
She butted him so hard that
his tummy split open and out jumped
her little kids, safe and sound.
Up jumped the big bad wolf, but
Mother Goat butted him so hard again that
he flew through the air and
he landed in the river.
That was the end of the big bad wolf,
and a good thing too.

Too much talk

A tortoise lived in a pond with two ducks.
He talked and talked
all day and all night.
It made the ducks cross but
whatever they said,
it made no difference.
The tortoise just went on talking.

One summer, the sun was very hot. The water in the pond dried up and the mud at the bottom of the pond began to crack.

"We must fly to the big lake where there is plenty of water," said the ducks.

"Take me with you," said the tortoise.

"Can you fly?" said the ducks.
"I can learn," said the tortoise.
"You have no wings," said the ducks,
"so we can't teach you to fly.
We will have to go without you."

"Wait," cried the tortoise.
"I have an idea."
He pulled a big stick from
the bottom of the pond.
"If each of you holds on to one end,"
said the tortoise,
"I can hold on to the middle and
then you can take me with you."

"Very well," said the ducks,
"but you must hold on tight and not talk."
"I won't talk," said the tortoise.
So the ducks each picked up
an end of the stick and
they flew off to find the lake.
The tortoise hung down and
said nothing.

They flew over trees and
they flew over gardens.
One little boy looked up into the sky.
"Look there," he cried. "Come and see.
The ducks are carrying a bag of washing."

The tortoise was cross.
He was **not** a bag of washing.
He was the first flying tortoise.
"I must tell him," he thought
and began to say, "I'm . . ."
when down he fell, down
                        and down
                            and down.

Until plop, he fell
into a basket of washing.
The boy's mother was very cross.
"That muddy tortoise has made
all my washing dirty," she said.
But the boy was very pleased
to have a new pet.
So the tortoise lived happily
in the garden for ever after.
But from that day to this
he has not talked to anyone.